Original title:
Galaxy Giggles

Copyright © 2025 Creative Arts Management OÜ
All rights reserved.

Author: Adrian Caldwell
ISBN HARDBACK: 978-1-80567-775-8
ISBN PAPERBACK: 978-1-80567-896-0

Humor in the Void

In the vastness, stars play tricks,
Wobbling like a bowl of ticks.
Planets toss around their hats,
While comets dance with playful spats.

Asteroids giggle, zoom and whizz,
No one knows just what that is.
Black holes hide with silly grins,
Sucking up all the airy sins.

Twinkling Teases

Meteor showers toss in jest,
Whizzing by as if they're blessed.
Jupiter winks with a great big smile,
While Mercury spins in a dizzying style.

Uranus rolls, a joker's spree,
Makes Saturn laugh, oh can't you see?
Stars chuckle softly, a cosmic crowd,
Whispering secrets, laughing loud.

Cosmic Capers

Galaxies swirl in a jolly spin,
Kites made of stardust they grin.
Nebulas flutter like fancy doves,
Loving the jokes from the stars above.

Planets race, a playful chase,
Each one vying for the silliest face.
A dance-off in the chilly night,
With jovial jests that feel just right.

Celestial Pranks

The sun pokes fun, a hot delight,
While solar flares leap in excitement's flight.
Astro-kids giggle with every spin,
As laughter echoes from deep within.

Rings of Saturn, they swirl and twirl,
Planets share a secret whirl.
Comets tease, sailing by with glee,
In this cosmic circus just wait and see!

Comet's Flair

A comet zooms with a bright, swift tail,
It winks at stars, leaving a glowing trail.
Jupiter chuckles, its storms in a spin,
While Saturn's rings dance, laughing within.

The asteroids giggle, tumbling in space,
As meteors leap, in a playful race.
Mars makes a joke, with its playful red,
And Venus joins in, with a twinkle ahead.

Moonbeam Mirth

Moonbeams bounce off the lakes like a game,
The night air is full of a frolicking flame.
Crickets join in with their rhythmic song,
While owls hoot softly, "We're right, not wrong!"

Stars raise their glasses, a toast in delight,
For laughter that sparkles throughout the night.
The clouds play tag, drifting light as a feather,
Shooting star wishes are crafted together.

Starlight Smiles

Starlight twinkles, a cheeky glow,
Winking like friends who put on a show.
Clusters of laughter, they swirl and twirl,
While galaxies giggle, a cosmic swirl.

Nebulae chuckle, all fluffy and bright,
Filling the universe with sheer delight.
As planets spin stories of their own charm,
They sparkle and shine, keeping us warm.

Quasar Quips

A quasar shouts, "Here I am, so bold!"
With jokes electric, and stories retold.
It zips through the void, a humor parade,
While black holes snicker, in shadows they fade.

Shooting stars laugh, in a whimsical flight,
As comets pull pranks, adding to the night.
With every twinkle, a giggle takes flight,
In this vast cosmic stage, what sheer delight!

Laughter in Lightyears

In the vastness of space, a comet sneezes,
Stars twinkle bright, as the cosmos teases.
An alien juggles, green and round,
While moons roll around making silly sounds.

A black hole giggles, it swallows a song,
Echoes of laughter, bouncing along.
Planets spin in circles, dizzy with cheer,
As rockets zoom past with a playful sneer.

Universal Jesters

Orbiting planets, each tell a tale,
Of goofy antics and cosmic rail.
Meteorites dance in a wobbly line,
Shooting stars wink, they're feeling just fine.

A space clown floats, with balloons in tow,
Tickling the stars, putting on a show.
Saturn's rings jingle, like bells in the night,
A symphony of laughter in the starlit flight.

Mirrored Mirth

In the mirror of space, reflections play,
Galactic giggles brighten the day.
Distant galaxies share a cosmic jest,
As stardust tickles, the universe rests.

Nebulas swirl, with colors so bold,
Painting chuckles in stories untold.
A cosmic mirror, with each shining face,
Reveals the humor in this vast space.

Orbiting Smiles

Around each star, a smile does weave,
Creating connections that never deceive.
Asteroids chuckle, they play hide and seek,
While shooting stars giggle, they streak down the peak.

In harmony, comets dance in delight,
Tickling the cosmos, it feels so right.
Gravity's pull can't stifle the fun,
As laughter bursts forth, a race never run.

Stellar Whims

In the night sky, stars play hide and seek,
Laughing out loud, they're quite the sneak.
Planets spin tales of cotton candy,
While comets prance, oh so dandy.

Meteorites tickle the sleepy moon,
Joking around, they hum a tune.
Galactic friends in a dance so bright,
Twinkling together, what a sight!

Sip of Stardust

With a spoonful of dreams and a dash of cheer,
I sip from the cosmos, my giggles appear.
Nebulas swirl in a fizzy delight,
Bubbles of laughter float in the night.

Saturn wears rings made of spun sugar,
While hiccuping stars dance with a swagger.
I twirl and I swirl in this cosmic brew,
Each sip a chuckle, each giggle anew!

Cosmic Cackles

Jupiter hops with a silly caper,
Making the moons drop their dessert paper.
A black hole yawns, but don't be alarmed,
It just swallows jokes and gets nicely charmed.

Silly comets zoom past in a race,
Playing tag with clouds in outer space.
With bursts of laughter, they scatter and flee,
In a universe where fun is the key!

Celestial Pantomime

Stars mime the stories of worlds untold,
Acting out wonders, both bright and bold.
The sun winks warmly, a playful tease,
While planets giggle, swaying with ease.

Cosmic jesters juggle asteroids high,
Tickling the void with a wink and a sigh.
Every light-year a chuckle, a rollicking ride,
In the theater of space, where fun can't hide!

Witty Cosmos

Stars twinkle with a cheeky grin,
Meteors race, it's a wild spin.
Planets dance in a merry line,
Jupiter jests, "I'm feeling fine!"

Saturn's rings jingle, what a show,
Uranus chuckles, "I'm in the know!"
Cosmic jokes float in the deep,
While comets prance, no time for sleep.

Laughter Through the Constellations

Orion's belt is quite a sight,
But oh, those stars are filled with light!
They share a joke with every spark,
Creating hilarity in the dark.

Little Leo roars with glee,
While Scorpius stings playfully.
They tease the night with starry pranks,
Galactic giggles in their ranks.

Playful Echoes

Echoes bounce from star to star,
"Did you hear that?" "Oh, how bizarre!"
Waves of laughter travel fast,
Cosmic fun is meant to last.

In the silence, you might see,
The moon winks at you with glee.
With every twinkle, take a chance,
Join the universe's dance.

Comet's Comedy

A comet zooms with a bright flare,
"Oh no," it says, "Too much hair!"
It spirals down with a goofy spin,
Leaving a trail of cosmic grin.

Asteroids roll, trying to run,
Falling stars just want some fun.
In the wide expanse, laughter beams,
As space unfolds its wittiest dreams.

Cosmic Curiosity

In the sky, a comet flies,
With a tail that tickles, oh what a surprise.
Planets spin in a merry dance,
While moons chuckle in a cosmic trance.

Stars wink and share a silly glee,
Shooting giggles just for me.
Asteroids bounce with a playful cheer,
As laughter echoes from year to year.

Planetary Puns

Mars told Venus, 'You're such a flame!'
While Earth rolled its eyes at the cosmic game.
Jupiter joked, 'I'm big, what a sight!'
While saturn's rings danced day and night.

Neptune swam in a punny sea,
Said, 'Why don't shells ever agree?'
Comets come by with a wink and a twist,
Bringing laughter that's hard to resist.

Stellar Snickers

A star shines bright with a cheeky grin,
'Why did the sun get a giggle within?'
Because it found some planets in a spin,
And they all laughed as the fun did begin.

Constellations play hide-and-seek,
As meteors crack jokes, so funny and sleek.
Galaxies swirl with a jolly shout,
For humor's the rocket that spins us about.

Lightyears of Laughter

In a black hole, jokes get sucked,
But space-time keeps giggles unplucked.
Every lightyear brings a new silly tale,
As UFOs swoop down, eager to hail.

Astro-bunnies hop with delight,
As UFOs zoom in the deep starry night.
Nebulas shimmer with colorful jest,
In the universe's humor, we're truly blessed.

Milky Way Mischief

Stars dance in a swirl, so bright,
Planets play hide and seek at night.
Comets giggle as they zoom,
In this cosmic, playful room.

Jupiter's jokes make Saturn grin,
While little moons spin round in spin.
Nebulas puff with laughter loud,
While stardust prances, oh so proud.

Asteroids chuckle on their way,
Bumping and bouncing, come what may.
Cosmic critters join the fun,
Under the smiles of the glowing sun.

Laughter echoes through the void,
In the universe, we're employed.
Mischief sparks from each bright light,
In this boundless, giggling night.

Serendipity in Space

Floating through the starry dance,
Planets twirl, they take a chance.
Meteor showers bring delight,
As they tumble, oh what a sight!

Aliens gather, they can't resist,
Trading their jokes, they twist and twist.
Gravity pulls them toward delight,
Making giggles that touch the night.

Wormholes wiggle with glee, oh so sly,
As astronauts chuckle and just pass by.
Time folds up and laughter springs,
In the cosmos, joy is king.

Starlit paths of laughter spun,
In this expanse, we all are one.
Serendipity in every star,
Finding humor near and far.

Gravitational Guffaws

In the pull of a black hole's charm,
Cosmic beings link arm in arm.
Tickled by the gravitational play,
Spinning merrily all the way.

Planets wobble and sway with cheer,
As the universe pulls us near.
Light beams tickle all in flight,
Filling the void with pure delight.

Supernovas burst with glee,
In the vastness, a funny spree.
Radiation dances with a grin,
Tickling space from within.

The comets leave trails of mirth,
As laughter echoes throughout the Earth.
In the void, we find our cause,
Finding joy in gravitational guffaws.

Celestial Conga

Stars align for a cosmic show,
In the dark, they twist and flow.
A conga line of cosmic cheer,
With each twinkle, we giggle here.

Asteroids bump with a joyful beat,
In the vast expanse, we stamp our feet.
Saturn spins with rings so wide,
While planets shuffle side by side.

Galactic beings join the dance,
In the sparkle, they take a chance.
With laughter echoing through the night,
They swirl and twirl in pure delight.

From Nova's bounce to Pluto's jig,
The universe laughs, it's all so big.
Join the conga, don't be shy,
In this cosmic dance, we'll soar and fly!

Whimsies of the Universe

In the cosmos, cats on a spree,
Chasing comets, wild and free.
With twinkling eyes and a goofy dance,
They leap and prance, as if by chance.

Asteroids waltz, with a clumsy grace,
While alien frogs make a funny face.
Planets giggle as they spin round,
In a cosmic circus, joy abound.

Nebulas puff out colorful smoke,
Funny little puffs that twist and poke.
Stars throw confetti, oh what a sight,
Shining with laughter in the night.

Uranus wears a hat, quite absurd,
While Mars whistles tunes that are simply heard.
In this vast playground, mirth on display,
The universe chuckles in its playful way.

Laughter Between the Stars

Bouncing moons, in a merry race,
Tickling comets, a cosmic chase.
Jovial giants clap with delight,
As laughter echoes through the night.

Little moons play peek-a-boo,
Hiding behind clouds, oh so blue.
Orbits twist while planets grin,
Even black holes chuckle within.

Shooting stars go zooming past,
Filling the sky with giggles vast.
With each burst of light and sound,
Joy in darkness will always abound.

In this arena of twinkling fun,
The universe dances, a raucous run.
With every twirl and every spin,
The stars shoot laughter; let it begin!

Radiant Reflections

Mirrors of starlight shimmer and shine,
Laughing together, a cosmic line.
Reflections of joy in the space so wide,
Bursting with giggles, they can't hide.

Quasars blink in rhythmic play,
Telling secrets in a silly way.
Pulsars tap their toes to a beat,
As the universe dances on joyful feet.

Galaxies spin with a whirl and a twirl,
Comets join in, ready to unfurl.
In this radiant show of delight,
Stars share jokes through the endless night.

Witty whispers ride on solar winds,
Wobbly universes make funny spins.
With every twinkling, with every grin,
The cosmos chuckles, let the fun begin!

Celestial Rapture

Clouds of stardust swirl with flair,
Painting the sky, without a care.
Planets crack jokes, oh what a sight,
As they spin in unison, laughing bright.

Silly space whales sing in harmony,
Splashing through stars, wild and free.
Meteor showers like fireworks fall,
Laughter erupts, a cosmic call.

Jupiter's storms start a playful fight,
While Saturn's rings spin in pure delight.
Every twinkle holds a tale to share,
Of adventures past, floating in air.

With every twinkling, the night ignites,
The universe giggles; such pure delights.
In this grand spectacle, joy soars high,
With whispers and laughter echoing in the sky.

Celestial Echoes of Laughter

In the night sky, stars play tricks,
Winking at us, like cosmic flicks.
Planets spin in silly dance,
While comets giggle in a trance.

Meteor showers make us grin,
As alien jokes twirl and spin.
Laughter bounces off the moon,
While space critters hum a tune.

Cosmic pranks soar through the void,
Creating joy that's never coy.
Black holes burp, and we all chuckle,
Every twinkle's a playful huddle.

In this vast and cheerful space,
Laughter paints a bright embrace.
Stars align for fun tonight,
Creating giggles, pure delight.

Orbiting Humor

Around the sun, we spin and sway,
Jokes like solar flares at play.
Venus makes a teasing face,
While Saturn wears a silly grace.

Asteroids throw a prank or two,
While laughing stars peek out anew.
Jupiter joins with a booming laugh,
It's the silliest cosmic staff!

Orbiting worlds share hearty glee,
As starships buzz with jubilee.
Galactic goofs fill the night,
Creating joy in every flight.

Comets crash with laughter loud,
A cosmic playground, oh so proud.
Every twinkling light's a smile,
In this universe, fun's worthwhile.

Stardust Smirks

Whispers of stardust make us chuckle,
As space kittens pounce and snuggle.
Nebulae giggle, swirling bright,
While quirky beings dance in flight.

Silly shadows in the dark,
Filling night skies with playful spark.
Supernovae burst with glee,
Sharing smiles with you and me.

Planets tease with gentle whirls,
As cosmic humor twirls and swirls.
Twinkling stars play hide and seek,
While voids echo with a squeak.

Galaxies twirl in joyful jest,
Turning nights into a fest.
Every laugh a starlit beam,
Creating a cosmic, bright dream.

Galactic Joyride

Hop on board a starry ride,
With laughter flowing like a tide.
Spacecraft zip with giddy cheer,
As we float on stardust, my dear.

Waltzing comets tease and spin,
While hitchhikers laugh, join in.
Bouncing off the Saturn rings,
We dance along while the cosmos sings.

A meteor with a funny hat,
Jokes about a cosmic cat.
Shooting stars flash in delight,
Lighting up our playful night.

Galaxies swirl in endless fun,
Every joke under the sun.
In this vast expanse, we cheer,
A joyful trip, with friends so near.

Moonbeam Merriment

In the sky where comets zoom,
Stars tickle laughter, bright as bloom.
Planets spin in playful chase,
While meteors dance in outer space.

Jupiter spins with a silly grin,
A wacky world where fun begins.
Saturn's rings are hula hoops,
As laughter echoes through the loops.

Nebulae burst with colors bold,
Making jokes of cosmic gold.
A supernova's giggle bright,
Lights up the dark with pure delight.

The cosmos sings with whimsy's charm,
As stardust winks like a lucky charm.
With each twinkle, chuckles grow,
In this universe of joy and glow.

Laughing Light Years

Across the void, a chuckle flies,
As light years pass with teasing sighs.
A star explodes in a fit of fun,
While asteroids race, each one a pun.

Wormholes twist with giddy glee,
Launching laughter through space and spree.
Aliens play with bouncing balls,
And silly shadows stretch on walls.

With every tick of time's sweet clock,
Galactic giggles around the block.
The universe winks, a prankster true,
As starlight dances, just for you.

So strap on your space boots, join the play,
In a cosmic carnival, come what may.
The laughter of light years makes us free,
In a universe full of jubilee.

Cosmic Capers

In the cradle of night, stars delight,
Doing somersaults, oh what a sight!
With little suns that skip and bounce,
And moonlit beams that twist and flounce.

Galaxies spin in a comic dance,
Inviting us all to join the prance.
Black holes giggle, swirling with flair,
As quirky quasars play tricks in the air.

Starlings leap from one star to another,
Singing tunes like no other.
With each caper, the cosmos laughs,
Turning dull moments into warm halves.

So let's soar through the cosmic air,
In a whirlwind of joy, without a care.
For in this universe, wild and wide,
Laughter reigns where mysteries abide.

Celestial Comedy Show

Welcome all to the galactic stage,
Where stars tell tales, funny and sage.
Black holes roast with a comical spin,
As twinkling lights bellied laugh from within.

Aliens giggle, sporting big hats,
While planets play games like playful cats.
Meteor showers rain down smiles,
As the comets toss their quirky styles.

A stardust jester leaps through the air,
With a punchline that's beyond compare.
Cosmic dust carries the giggles wide,
In this comedy show, we all take pride.

So gather 'round for a stellar sight,
As the universe bursts with laughter bright.
For every joke spun from the skies,
Is a masterpiece under cosmic highs.

Whimsical Worlds Above

In the sky where stars play,
Planets dance the night away.
Jovial giants in moonlit hats,
Tickle comets and chat with cats.

Rockets zoom with silly grins,
Asteroids chuckle, share their sins.
Nebulas burst with sparkly cheer,
Whispers of laughter fill the sphere.

Fuzzy aliens skate on beams,
Wobbling wildly in their dreams.
Silly shadows waltz and spin,
Chasing light with gleeful grins.

Galactic games in cosmic nests,
Where merriment never rests.
Laughter echoes through the void,
In this realm where joy's enjoyed.

Jovial Journeys Across the Cosmos

Spaceships slide on buttered trails,
Hitching rides on comet tails.
Stars giggle as they bounce and twirl,
While planets smirk and dance and swirl.

With every leap, the laughter grows,
Sing along with meteors' throes.
Shooting stars throw parties bright,
Celebrating in the velvet night.

Wormholes twist in silly hops,
As laughter travels, never stops.
Planets bounce like playful pups,
Celestial cheer that always ups.

Navigating joy through time,
Floating on this silly rhyme.
Through the cosmos, together we roam,
In this jolly, star-lit home.

Radiant Riddles in the Night

Shooting stars with winks and nods,
Crafting riddles like quirky gods.
Galaxies spin with a cheeky grin,
Finding laughter deep within.

Planets toss their playful jokes,
Jovial whispers from cosmic folks.
Witty words in the starry dark,
Lighting up the night like a spark.

Meteor showers rain down puns,
As the cosmic comedy runs.
Through the void, the giggles fly,
Tickling the universe nearby.

With each riddle, stars unfold,
Stories of joy waiting to be told.
In this absurd, sparkling sight,
Radiance glimmers, pure delight.

Quasar Quips

Quasars beam a zany light,
Sending chuckles through the night.
Cosmic beings with sparkling eyes,
Share their tales of silly highs.

Wobbling worlds spin round and round,
In this laughter-laden ground.
Twinkling stars play tag in streams,
While space pets chase their giggly dreams.

Each supernova bursts with cheer,
As laughter echoes far and near.
Galactic gags and cosmic jokes,
In this place where humor pokes.

Twisted time with a hearty laugh,
In this universe, we share the craft.
So join the fun in every quip,
As we ride on this joy-filled trip.

Giggling Stars in Orbit

Twinkling lights in the night,
Winking at tales of delight.
Planets spin with cheeky grace,
Who knew space could hold such space?

Asteroids play hide and seek,
Chasing dreams while planets peek.
Meteor showers burst with cheer,
Laughter echoing, crystal clear.

Dwarf stars jump and dance around,
In the cosmic playground, laughter's found.
With every flash, a giggle flies,
Through the darkened velvet skies.

Laughter Among the Comets

Comets trail like cotton candy,
Zooming past all things so dandy.
Whispers on solar winds so loud,
The universe appears so proud.

With tails that tickle and tease,
They dance through space with such ease.
A frolic of giggles in flight,
Turning the cosmos into a sight.

Orbiting moons join in the fun,
Bumping together, oh what a run!
A cosmic party in every direction,
Spreading smiles, a joyful connection.

Cosmic Serenade

In the distance, a melody plays,
A tune of laughter in cosmic rays.
Shooting stars join the quirky song,
Making the universe feel so strong.

Nebulae swirl with colors bright,
Creating giggles in wondrous light.
Spinning spirals, they sway and twirl,
In the arms of the starlit whirl.

Harmony echoes through the void,
As playful spirits sing, not coy.
With cosmic humor in the air,
The heavens dance without a care.

Dancing with the Distant Suns

Distant suns with golden beams,
Chase each other like childhood dreams.
Caught in a game, they laugh and spin,
A lighthearted race, let the fun begin!

Galactic whirlwinds swirl around,
Creating laughter that's profound.
Playful photons leap and glide,
In the comedy of the galactic ride.

Radiant rays in a cosmic jig,
Twirl and spin to music big.
In this stellar show, let joy ignite,
Dancing boldly in the starry night.

Starlit Laughter

In a sky of shimmering beams,
Stars play jokes, or so it seems.
A comet slips on cosmic ice,
We laugh together, isn't it nice?

Planets spin with wobbly grace,
Kidding each other in their race.
A meteor's dash, a twinkling tease,
Makes constellations giggle with ease.

Cosmic Chuckles

The sun winks at the cheeky moon,
As stardust dances to a silly tune.
Galaxies spin in a dizzy swirl,
Making every space traveler twirl.

Asteroids knock with playful might,
Playing tag, oh what a sight!
Nebulas puff out puffs of cheer,
Spreading laughter far and near.

The Joyful Nebula

In the clouds of colors bright,
Planets share jokes late at night.
Stars burst out in fits of glee,
Tickling space with whimsy spree.

Whirling comets toss confetti wide,
Encouraging laughter far and wide.
Each twinkle's giggle fills the air,
In a universe that loves to share.

Celestial Whispers

Whispers float on starlit air,
As constellations share their flair.
A shooting star, a silly song,
Reminds us that we all belong.

Galactic pranks and playful spins,
Bringing fun from where it begins.
Cosmic kites in a breezy flight,
Laughing with joy, a pure delight.

Whispers of Celestial Joy

In the night, stars play tricks,
Winking lights and silly flicks.
Planets dance with vibrant hues,
Making merry, sharing views.

Cosmic clowns in moonlit shoes,
Spinning tales, no chance to lose.
Asteroids toss, comets giggle,
In this dance, we all wiggle.

Galaxies hum a playful tune,
Tickling thoughts like a balloon.
Laughter echoes through the void,
In this joy, we are employed.

Stardust falls like sprinkles sweet,
Every chuckle, a tasty treat.
Light years stretch with every joke,
Making merry, never broke.

Twinkling Grins

Stars wear smiles, wide and bright,
Crafting giggles in the night.
Constellations swap their hats,
Dancing round like silly bats.

Meteors race, what a sight!
Who can break the speed of light?
Jovial moons roast marshmallows,
While Venus plays with furry fellows.

A universe of jests and cheers,
Jokes that span the stratosphere.
Black holes laugh with a deep glee,
Sucking in fun, endlessly.

Planets tease their orbit's place,
Round and round, a merry chase.
Twinkling grins all around us,
In this fun, we simply trust.

Nebula of Delight

In clouds of color, laughter swirls,
Brightening the cosmos' curls.
Puffy shapes that bounce around,
In this joy, we all are found.

Stars perform their silly plays,
Spotting comets on their ways.
Giggles echo off the moons,
Singing out delightful tunes.

Whirling galaxies do the cha-cha,
Underneath a glowing star.
Space is full of gleeful noise,
With every whim, we find our joys.

Cosmic chuckles, spark and shine,
Creating fun, so divine.
In this nebula of light,
Laughter dances through the night.

Laughter Among the Stars

Beneath the vault of twinkling dreams,
Laughter flows in silvery streams.
Together we find silly sights,
As jovial stars share their lights.

Supernovae burst with glee,
Painting worlds so wild and free.
Alien critters jest and play,
In their quirky, charming way.

Dance with comets, spin and twirl,
While Saturn's rings begin to whirl.
Tickled by the starlit glow,
In this joy, we all follow.

Funny sounds from black holes sing,
Creating joy, it's everything!
So lets embrace this cosmic cheer,
Laughter echoed far and near.

Playful Moonscape

In the night, the moons jump high,
Wobbling stars dance in the sky.
Planets wear their silliest hats,
While comets giggle like old cats.

Saturn spun in a twirly loop,
While Earthlings laughed with all their hoop.
Jupiter plays hide and seek,
Winking at those who dare peek.

Asteroids chuckle, rolling past,
Twirling in laughter, oh so fast.
Cosmic jokes shared with a grin,
As stardust tickles everyone's chin.

Nebulae burst with giggly cheer,
Creating chuckles far and near.
In this moonscape, fun takes flight,
Where every twinkle shines so bright.

Grins on Meteor Trails

Meteor showers paint the night,
Each one trailing jokes so bright.
With a whoosh and a fluffy tail,
They giggle like a breezy sail.

Stars are winking, what a sight,
As planets whirl in pure delight.
Zany bursts of laughter roam,
Across the sky, they call it home.

Saturn's ring is a hula hoop,
While Venus joins the lively troupe.
Galactic puns blast through the air,
As laughter echoes everywhere.

Galaxies swirl in a merry dance,
Spinning jokes, they'll take a chance.
In this cosmos, smiles collide,
On trails of stardust, pure joy slides.

Stellar Smiles Unbound

Stars align to form a grin,
While laughing comets speed on in.
With each blink, a joke appears,
Tickling hearts and giggling cheers.

Planets spin in dizzy rounds,
Creating joy in jumping sounds.
Cosmic clowns, they prance around,
In the vastness, laughter's found.

Asteroids toss confetti bright,
Each burst a spark of pure delight.
Nebulas gleam in colors bold,
Whispering secrets, yet untold.

With every wink and twinkling light,
The universe giggles deep in the night.
In a playful embrace, all around,
The essence of humor knows no bound.

Nova Nonsense

In the cosmos, where jesters play,
Nonsense blooms in a bright array.
Galactic giggles echo far,
As stellar puns take shape like a star.

Quasars flicker with silly jokes,
While lunar lanterns share their pokes.
Gravity pulls the laughter tight,
As meteors sparkle with delight.

Every planet has its quirk,
In this universe, smiles lurk.
Wacky orbits make hearts soar,
While stars trade jokes from core to core.

Supernovae burst with glee,
Unleashing joy like a wild spree.
In this cosmic carnival's glow,
Nonsense reigns—we let it flow.

Nebula Nonsense

In the cosmos, a star did wink,
While a comet danced, don't you think?
Black holes laugh like the universe's jest,
Pulling in tales, but never at rest.

Planets twirl in a playful race,
Saturn's rings spin with a silly grace.
Asteroids chuckle, bumping about,
In this silly space, there's no doubt.

Galaxies giggle, swirling with glee,
While moons play hide-and-seek with the sea.
A meteor shower brings jokes from afar,
Shooting stars whisper, "Wish on a bizarre!"

Join this romp where the night is bright,
In a playful universe, take flight.
With twinkling eyes and laughter loud,
The cosmos beckons us, fun and proud.

Celestial Chucklefest

In the void, a star tickles the night,
While the sun beams down with all its might.
Planets giggle as they spin around,
In this merry place where joy is found.

Cosmic critters bounce and play,
As dark matter gets caught in delay.
Jasmine comets leave trails of smiles,
Chasing starlight for endless miles.

Light-years traveled in fits of glee,
Each supernova bursts in a spree.
The Milky Way chuckles in rhyme,
While stardust dances, oh so sublime.

Join the fun, it's a blast to explore,
Where the universe plays and asks for more.
In this bright jamboree above,
Laughter's the language, so wear your glove.

Astral Antics

Amongst the stars, a prankster gleams,
Throwing wishes through cosmic beams.
With silver spaceships, they zoom and spin,
Laughing with joy, let the fun begin!

Galactic jesters jump and cheer,
Telling tales to the stars up here.
Comets wear hats tilted just so,
Shooting by, with a wink and a glow.

Asteroids bounce like playful pups,
Nibbling on stardust from silly cups.
Waves of laughter echo and flow,
In the vast playground of twinkling show.

Join the laughter, let yourself soar,
Where the universe smiles, forevermore.
With each twinkling star, each funny face,
It's a raucous world of joy and grace.

Universal Uproar

When planets collide in a clumsy dance,
Galactic giggles lead to a prance.
Cosmic balloons float and sway,
As suns ignite in a bright display.

Nebulas puff with colorful cheer,
Spreading joy that sparks the sphere.
Each quasar gives a cheeky laugh,
As gravity pulls the funny craft.

In this realm of whimsy and light,
Wormholes twist in sheer delight.
Pulsars play beats, a musical spree,
Echoing giggles endlessly.

So strap in tight for this wild ride,
Where the universe's laughter won't subside.
Each flicker and flash, a sign to savor,
In this cosmic fun, we find our favor.

Jovial Journeys

Through the stars, we dance and sway,
With rainbow comets leading the way.
Laughter echoes in the cosmic seas,
As aliens juggle with moonlit cheese.

Meteorites play hopscotch in style,
While Saturn spins round with a cheeky smile.
Planets twirl under a shimmering light,
Tickling each other all throughout the night.

Galactic dust bunnies bounce off the walls,
Shooting stars whispering funny calls.
Wishing wells teem with bright, silly dreams,
As stardust bursts into giggling beams.

Join the fun, lose track of time,
In this swirling realm, it's all in rhyme.
With joy and laughter breaching the skies,
Every twinkle wears a grin that flies.

Celestial Smiles

Above in the night, twinkling bright,
Giggles echo in the starry light.
Planets roll with a clumsy grace,
Chasing each other in a playful race.

Asteroids dressed in polka dot clothes,
Wiggle and dance like nobody knows.
Galactic critters with silly hats,
Hop aboard space buses, giving high fives to cats.

Moons shimmer with a playful wink,
As cosmic cupcakes float and sink.
Stars trade jokes while spinning around,
Filling the silence with joy unbound.

At playful picnics on fluffy space trails,
Laughter and friendship, the wind that sails.
With each chortle, the cosmos sings,
In this merry dance, joy takes wings.

Comet's Wink

A comet zooms with a playful tease,
Whirling through space, a breeze with ease.
Winking at stardust, sharing a laugh,
In the cosmic studio, they draw a path.

Shooting stars line up for a race,
Hilarious faces in every case.
Saturn's rings tangle, creating a mess,
But laughter erupts, a cosmic caress.

Uranus giggles with a funny twist,
While Venus insists she cannot be missed.
Galactic tales of playful fights,
Light up the heavens on sleepless nights.

Jokes traded on solar flares' wings,
While space critters share silly flings.
As they laugh till their orbits align,
The universe hums a joyful rhyme.

Cosmic Revelry

In a playful cosmos, the laughter spills,
Over moonlit mountains and starlit hills.
Planets exchange their goofy tales,
As nebulae rumble like silly gales.

A rocket ship trips in a giggling flight,
Crashing softly in a bubbly light.
Cosmic confetti rains from the skies,
Wrapped in the warmth of cheerful sighs.

Alien friends throw a party all night,
Every twirl and whirl brings pure delight.
With ice cream meteors and punch that shines,
They toast to friendship, their love aligns.

Stargazers chuckle under a rainbow hue,
Counting each chuckle as dreams come true.
In this realm of wonder, joy takes the stage,
A vibrant laughter, the heart of the age.

Jovial Heights

In the sky, where comets dance,
Laughter echoes at every chance.
Stars wear hats, bright and silly,
Making the night so very frilly.

Planets play hide and seek,
Around the sun, they spin and peek.
Oh, what joy, a cosmic game,
Where laughter's spark ignites a flame.

Playful Stardust

Sprinkled sparkles, tickles abound,
With shooting stars that make a sound.
Winking moons with cheeky grins,
Invite us all to join the spins.

Galactic giggles, bright and loud,
Draw in the comets, round and proud.
In this realm of goofy cheer,
Every twinkle whispers, "Come here!"

Cosmic Amusement

Juggling meteors up above,
Twinkling like they're in love.
Every asteroid has a joke,
In this realm where mischief's woke.

Silly rabbits on Saturn's rings,
Bouncing high as laughter sings.
With every wobble, a giggle spills,
Chasing joy down nebula hills.

Nebulistic Nonsense

Clouds of color, whimsically bright,
Making a ruckus in the night.
Giggles echo through the void,
Imagination never toyed.

Whirling galaxies, what a sight,
With all the wonders taking flight.
As we twirl through this radiant spree,
Join the fun, just you and me!

Harmony in the Heavens

Stars wink and poke, a jolly tease,
Planets spin with a silly breeze.
Comets dance with a glittery swirl,
While asteroids chase in a cosmic twirl.

Nebulas giggle, painting the night,
Space dust chuckles, glowing so bright.
Moonbeams laugh, bouncing off dreams,
Creating a symphony of playful schemes.

Wormholes yawn, stretch wide with glee,
The Milky Way hums a tune, carefree.
In this vast place, joy takes flight,
Laughter echoes through the dark night.

As meteors whiz with a wink and a grin,
The cosmos invites us to join in the spin.
With every twinkle, we share a jest,
In the heart of the night, we're truly blessed.

Radiance of Whimsy

Bubbles of starlight float on by,
Jovial rays spark up the sky.
Puffy clouds wear silly hats,
Tickled by the sun, they giggle and chat.

A wink from Venus, a nudge from Mars,
Cosmic chuckles drift from far stars.
Shooting stars play hide and seek,
While space-time twists with a bubbly squeak.

Galactic gardens bloom with cheer,
Dancing flowers draw aliens near.
All around, the universe sings,
Of joyful tales and whimsical things.

Black holes spin with a mischievous play,
Swirling secrets that twirl away.
In the laughter of lightyears, we find our place,
In this whimsical cosmos, a joyous space.

Playful Pulsars

Pulsars thump with a joyful beat,
Sending signals, so lively and sweet.
Light-years away, the fun never ends,
As space buddies share their silly trends.

Neutron stars bounce like they're on a swing,
Gravity decides to join in the fling.
Orbiting planets join in the dance,
Underneath starlight's playful expanse.

Distant galaxies chuckle and sway,
In the vastness, they play hideaway.
Asteroids leap like popcorn in a pan,
Enjoying the freedom across the expanse.

In this realm of cosmic delight,
The universe giggles, shining so bright.
Together we twirl, through time and space,
Celebrating the joy in this radiant place.

Interstellar Merriment

Through the dark, the laughters soar,
A chorus of joy, we can't ignore.
Each twinkle a giggle, each flare a cheer,
In the arms of space, we have no fear.

Bright moons shine with a playful glare,
While stardust sprinkles laughter in the air.
Galaxies whirl, spinning wild and free,
In this grand jest, come dance with me!

Radiating humor from every side,
Even comets take a wild ride.
Sparkly snippets of cosmic bliss,
In a universe painted with giggly mist.

So let us journey, past planets and suns,
Discover the fun in celestial runs.
With laughter entwined through the vast unknown,
The interstellar mirth felt in every zone.

Celestial Jests

In the night's vast playground, stars play hide and seek,
Planets spin in laughter, their colors bold and chic.
Little comets race, with tales of silly sun,
As cosmic winds blow giggles, oh what endless fun!

Saturn spins its rings, a circus in the sky,
While nearby Mars is blushing, as the asteroids fly by.
Jupiter's great belly, shakes with every roar,
As moons dance around him, always wanting more!

With each twinkling beacon, a wink and cheeky grin,
Nebulas chuckle softly, inviting us to spin.
Galactic puns abound, in colors bright and bold,
The universe is joking, in a story to be told!

So reach for the night's canvas, paint it bright with mirth,
Each star a little joker, spread joy across the Earth.
In this endless theater, where laughter finds its space,
The cosmos bursts with jests, a shimmering embrace.

Starry Serenades

Underneath bright twinkles, you'll hear a soft refrain,
Singing stars in concert, their joy is quite insane.
Moonbeams laugh in whispers, as shadows tap their toes,
Dancing on the stardust, where the happiest wind blows.

Orbits become rhythms, in this cosmic cabaret,
Each satellite a soloist, that charms and loves to play.
With every gentle spiral, laughter echoes wide,
As the universe composes, its joyful starry guide.

From meteoric maracas, to planets' boisterous beat,
There's humor in the harmony, in every loveable feat.
The constellation's laughter, lights the velvety void,
With chuckles in the cosmos, enchantment is employed.

So sway to the starlight, let your spirit soar and sway,
Join the merry symphony, let your worries drift away.
For in this vast expanse, where giggles intertwine,
The universe is singing, and all the stars align!

Laughter on Astral Winds

Breath of cosmic breezes brings giggles from afar,
Whispers of the cosmos drift down on us like stars.
Constellations chuckle softly, in patterns made of light,
As we catch their jests and notes, floating through the night.

In this wacky universe, black holes wear a hat,
Flirting with the stardust, oh how the comets chat!
And each weird planet dances, with a wobble and a spin,
As the galaxies unite, in a merry, twinkling din.

Jumping through the asteroids, they toss a wink or two,
Creating cosmic mischief, with every boundless view.
The vastness holds the secrets, of laughter never ceased,
In this realm of whimsical, our joy has been released.

So let's embrace the stardust, let our spirits lift and glide,
On winds of fun and frolic, laughter as our guide.
In this magical expanse, with smiles that warm the night,
The universe is chuckling, and everything feels right.

Shooting Star Shenanigans

On the cusp of midnight, wishes zoom and zip,
Shooting stars in mischief, on a playful trip.
Each trail a giggle glowing, in a burst of bright delight,
Echoing across the cosmos, painting dark with light.

With their jolly hijinks, they streak across the sky,
Tickling the sly old moon, with a cheeky little sigh.
The tail of every comet, ripe with laughter's spark,
As they blend in cosmic chaos, leaving joyful marks.

In a race beyond the planets, the starry fellows prance,
Cosmic clowns in costumes, who beckon us to dance.
With every twirl and twist, they invite us to explore,
A universe of wonders, bursting open every door.

So here among the stardust, let our laughter ring out clear,

Chasing whimsical adventures, with friends both far and near.
For in this joyous starlight, where every heart can play,
Shooting stars are winking: let's seize the night and stay!

Tickling the Milky Way

Stars twinkle like they're in a jest,
Comets race by, wearing their best.
Planets chuckle in their own spin,
While moons play tag and join in the din.

Wormholes waddle, what a sight,
Black holes giggle, oh what a fright!
Asteroids bounce like they're in a game,
While space dust dances, never the same.

Nebulas puff with colors bright,
As stardust sprinkles the deep, dark night.
Laughter echoes in the cosmic dance,
As meteors tumble in a wobbly prance.

So here we float in a silly spree,
In this vast playground of mystery.
With a wink and a nod, we spread our cheer,
For in the universe, fun's always near.

Humor in the Dark Void

In the quiet of space where shadows reign,
Asteroids snicker, causing a chain.
Comets with jokes streak through the night,
While planets giggle, what a delight!

The void is filled with whimsical cheer,
As stars share puns we barely hear.
Celestial bodies engage in jest,
Making the cosmos a lively fest.

A black hole cracks a joke so sly,
While meteors burst like fireworks in the sky.
With laughter echoing through the vastness wide,
Even supernovae can't keep inside!

So while we drift in the dark, so grand,
Let's join the fun, take a cosmic stand.
In this universe endless, let spirit soar,
For humor's the language at the core.

Celestial Follies

On Saturn's rings, they set up a show,
With giggles and gags, and a bright glow.
Jovian jesters leap with glee,
As Martian clowns serve tea with three.

Bouncing through clusters, so silly and free,
Dancing on stardust, as light as can be.
Let's twirl with asteroids, spin with delight,
In this cosmic carnival, all through the night.

Space whales sing in a tune quite absurd,
While shooting stars trumpet, oh what a herd!
Planets play pranks, spinning tales so wild,
In this vast nursery, rebirth is styled.

So come take a trip on this playful ride,
In celestial follies, we stand side by side.
With laughter in starlight, we boldly explore,
In the universe's heart, there's always more.

Galactic Grins

In a universe brimming with laughter and light,
Stars share their smiles, oh what a sight!
Planets toss pies from their moonlit rings,
While rovers dance, doing silly things.

Little saturns wobble, a clumsy ballet,
As comets play tricks, streaming away.
In the cosmic playground, there's never a frown,
With giggling starlings all over the town.

Nebulas swirl in a colorful spree,
Painting the skies, how joyful are we!
They whisper sweet secrets of jokes from afar,
In this cosmic circus, under a star.

So let's float along, with joy as our kin,
For the cosmos is grinning, let the fun begin!
From quasars to planets, with glee we ascend,
In this vast universe, giggles never end.

Jovian Jest

In swirling storms of gas so grand,
A jester floats with laughter planned.
With lightning jokes and giggling moons,
They dance to the tune of cosmic tunes.

A comet tail wags like a dog,
Chasing stars through an interstellar fog.
Planets chuckle in playful spins,
While meteors wink and share their sins.

Saturn's rings jingle with delight,
As asteroids tumble in a playful fight.
Jovian jesters on fun-filled quests,
Make the night sky their joyous fest.

With playful pranks and starry cheers,
They tickle the cosmos, erase our fears.
Among the twinkling lights they thrive,
In the laughter of space, we come alive.

Celestial Riddles

A curious star with a twinkling eye,
Ponders riddles that flutter by.
Why did the moon break up with the sun?
Too bright, too hot, and no more fun!

Little aliens with silly hats,
Tell tales of Martians chasing cats.
What's green and loves to shout 'Hooray'?
A rocket frog jumping into the fray!

In the vacuum, echoes of laughter ring,
As planets giggle at the tales they bring.
A snickering comet plays peek-a-boo,
While stars wink back, "Hey, we see you!"

With riddles that bounce from here to afar,
The cosmos is filled with joyful spar.
Through laughter and wit, we find our way,
In the grand play of night and day.

Starlit Satire

In the shadow of a twinkling bright,
Comedians gather for a cosmic night.
With jokes about black holes and light-speed gaffes,
They leave the universe roaring with laughs.

A planet declared, "I'm round, it's true!"
"Who needs a shape? It's me, it's you!"
Saturn grinned with rings quite wide,
"Start a band! Let's bring the tide!"

Galaxies spin with a twist of fate,
As stardust folks wait for their plate.
With humor that swirls among the stars,
The whole Milky Way cheers with guffaws.

In this cosmic jest, they all unite,
With laughter echoing deep in the night.
So raise a glass, here's to the fun,
In the universe where jokes are spun!

Radiant Revelations

Amidst the glow of a rosy hue,
A quirky sun reveals what's true.
Why do asteroids hate playing peek?
Because they always fall—oh, the cheek!

A starball bounces on a rainbow beam,
Tumbling through the celestial theme.
"Hey, universe, what's your favorite song?"
"Anything but that slow-moan throng!"

With laughter trails left far behind,
All cosmic beings playfully unwind.
From meteors that sing to comets that dance,
They share the joy with every glance.

As light-years pass and planets sway,
Radiant revelations crinkle the way.
In this grand expanse, let's join the spree,
And cherish laughter in our cosmic sea.

Lightheartedness in Space

Stars are twinkling with glee,
Cosmic chuckles dance carefree.
A planet slips on a bright green sock,
And moons giggle on each tick-tock.

Asteroids bounce in a silly race,
While comets wear a silly face.
Beyond the dark, there's laughter loud,
As space worms wiggle, so proud!

In orbits, joy begins to swirl,
As stars make jokes that softly twirl.
With every burst of starlit light,
They bring muffled giggles through the night.

Nebulas shimmer in dreamy hues,
Creating smiles, like happy crews.
In the vastness, mirth takes flight,
A universe filled with pure delight.

Comedic Constellations

Orion trips on his own belt,
With each tumble, more laughter's felt.
The Big Dipper steals the show,
Dancing friends with a cheeky glow.

Pegasus pranks with a playful swoop,
He tickles the stars while forming a loop.
Laughter rings through the cosmic air,
As Draco jokes with a charming flair.

Stars play hopscotch in the night,
Drawing shapes that spark delight.
A clown-faced comet whizzes by,
Leaving trails as he starts to fly.

In this dance of light and mirth,
Each twinkle knows its happy worth.
From far and wide, let joy arise,
In the fabric where laughter lies.

Joy Across the Universe

In the void, laughter erupts,
A star shines bright as it interrupts.
Planets giggle, a merry cheer,
As funny faces appear near.

Quasars hum a silly tune,
As they waft in the cosmic noon.
A burst of light with a wink,
Belly laughs from the links they link.

Cosmic jesters throw a show,
With meteors that dance below.
Jovial gales twist around,
Where joy in stardust can be found.

Each galaxy spreads tales of fun,
With whispers of laughter 'neath the sun.
In every corner, smiles grow,
A playful universe in tow.

Celestial Pranks

The sun plays tricks with a wink,
It hides behind clouds for a playful clink.
Moons spin yarns as shadows cast,
Making time fly incredibly fast.

Martian giggles soar high above,
With wacky antics they truly love.
Saturn's rings laugh as they twirl,
Spinning tales that make stars swirl.

A rocket sneezes, sending sparks,
As aliens join in and make their marks.
Echoing jokes through the starry gates,
Creating grins that eternity creates.

With every twinkle, a prank unfolds,
In the cosmos, humor proudly holds.
As the night sky bursts with cheers,
The universe chuckles through the years.

Jovial Innovations of the Cosmos

Stars squeak like rubber toys,
In the void, they make some noise.
Planets dance with comical flair,
Twinkling lights in a cosmic fair.

Nebulas puff like cotton candy,
With colors bright and oh so dandy.
Asteroids tumble, a clumsy show,
Who knew space could bring such glow?

Comets race in funny hats,
Leaving trails as they zoom past.
Galaxies spin like dizzy toys,
Creating laughter with the cosmos' poise.

In this vast, imaginative space,
Joy rides through each starry trace.
The universe plays its jest,
A playful whimsy that we love best.

Aha! Insights from the Infinite.

Planets sip on cosmic tea,
While moons gossip, wild and free.
Asteroids, with winks, they roll,
In this oddball universe, what's the goal?

Shooting stars spill silly dreams,
Twinkling like those moonlit beams.
Galactic whispers, tickles and grins,
Spark laughter where wonder begins.

Quasars giggle, bursting bright,
With secrets hid in beams of light.
Galaxies shuffle in grand parade,
finite fun that never fades.

Black holes boast of cosmic dives,
With alien pranks that come alive.
Endless fun in the astral sea,
Oh, the joy of this cosmic spree!

Starlit Laughter

Stars trade jokes in twinkling tones,
While comets giggle in frosty moans.
Nebulas burst with glittering glee,
As they swirl in a whimsical spree.

Saturn's rings begin to sway,
As planets join the funny play.
An asteroid slips, doing a flip,
With laughter echoing on its trip.

Constellations, in quirky forms,
Bring silly shapes during storms.
Pulsars tickle the silken night,
Filling the sky with pure delight.

In this vibrant dance of light,
Each heartbeat twinkles, pure and bright.
The cosmos hums a joyful tune,
Filled with laughter that makes hearts swoon.

Cosmic Chuckles

Wormholes weave funny little tales,
As stardust tickles stellar trails.
Planets spin, a merry waltz,
In this universe, there's no faults.

Galactic giggles in endless night,
Where comets play and stars ignite.
The sun rolls over, bright and round,
In this circus, joy abounds.

Satellites wink with a knowing smirk,
As meteors skedaddle, what a perk!
Each moment sparkles with laughter sweet,
In the vast expanse where wonders meet.

Cosmos grins, with stars to share,
A realm of jokes beyond compare.
In stellar games where silliness thrives,
A playful verse that truly strives.

www.ingramcontent.com/pod-product-compliance
Lightning Source LLC
Chambersburg PA
CBHW051642160426
43209CB00004B/762